# TEACHER'S COMPANION
R.B. APPLETON

INITIUM

Text Copyright © 1915 Reginald Bainbridge Appleton
Foreword Copyright © 2024 Nigel Wetters Gourlay

ISBN 978-1-913725-08-2

Published by Nigel Gourlay, Ashworth House, Long Lane, Chapel-en-le-Frith, High Peak, SK23 0TF, United Kingdom
ngourlay@gmail.com

## PUBLISHER'S FOREWORD

The Direct Method, supremely espoused in the teaching practice of W.H.D. Rouse, reflecting a wider Edwardian movement amongst foreign-language acquisition, is still promoted during initial teacher training for Classicists in England, even in the third decade of the twenty-first century. Why should this be?

*Initium* by Reginald Bainbridge Appleton, an acolyte of Rouse at The Perse School in Cambridge, has long been studied by novices and veterans alike, a book which vexes as much as it illuminates, detailing the first year of Latin lessons for boys of twelve or thirteen years, boys who knew corporal punishment, and who could darkly joke in ancient languages about the cruelty of their schoolmaster. Almost immediately, teachers are confronted with an insurmountable difficulty, that these scruffy little Edwardian characters are receiving six Latin lessons a week, their initial year expanding to two or three in any modern school.

But before this, there is another boulder blocking the way forward. In the Preface to *Initium*, it is clear that the first twelve lessons are missing from that book, and teachers must refer to another book *The Teacher's Companion*, many years out of circulation, before they commence. This is the book you hold in your hands, and which previously has been available only to the most ardent book-collector.

I hope in re-publishing this small, important work, you will discover for yourself how the Direct Method fits into your teaching, cherishing the conversations with your students.

Nigel Gourlay, Christmas 2024

# INTRODUCTION

This *libellus* is intended for the teacher's use in connection with our beginners' Latin book, which should not be put into the hands of the class until the ground represented by the following twelve sections has been covered by purely oral work. These sections are a report of the first twelve lessons actually given to a class of beginners; it has seemed to us that by reproducing these as accurately as possible we shall provide a clearer indication of the early procedure upon the direct method than would be possible by any other means. Teachers need not of course cover each section in a single lesson; the class upon which these were tried was somewhat above average in intelligence. Most beginners will need rather more than twelve lessons for them.

## § 1.

**Who the Romans were, and why we learn Latin.** Brief remarks upon the influence of Rome on later civilization. Local remains. Influence of Latin language on English language. Spelling. Derivations. Roman literature.

**Roman Alphabet and Pronunciation.** This can be *explained* in a few minutes; it is *taught* by exacting extreme care during this and later lessons. For the reformed pronunciation see *Recommendations of the Classical Association on the teaching of Latin and Greek* (Murray, 1s.), Postgate's *How to pronounce Latin* (Bell, 1s.), or *The restored pronunciation of Greek and Latin*, by Arnold and Conway (Cambridge University Press, 1s.). Great care should be taken throughout with quantities, not neglecting hidden quantities. Westaway's *Latin quantity and accent* (Cambridge University Press, 3s.) is most useful on this subject.

**Grammar.** Sentence structure. Subject, predicate, object. Point out that in Latin most of the meaning is in the endings. In order to drive this home the endings of all words are, in the first portion of the *Initium* book, printed in different type.

This first lesson is, of course, conducted in English.

## § 2.

M. = master. P. = pupil.

M.     [rising from his chair] *Surgo.* This is repeated once or twice.

M.     [pointing at some bright boy] *Surge.* Boy rises, and master says *Surgis.*

         This is repeated with other boys. Then the master turns to the rest of the class, and, pointing at a boy told to rise, says *Surgit.*

M.     *Ego surgo.*
         [pointing to boy] *Surge! Tu surgis.*
         [looking at the class, but pointing to the boy] *Ille surgit.*

         The class then repeat *Surgo,*
                                       *surgis,*
                                       *surgit;*
         then                 *Ego surgo,*
                                       *tu surgis,*
                                       *ille surgit.*

M.     [rising] *Quid facio?* The meaning of this was at once guessed from the intonation, and the correct answer *Surgis* came from several of the brighter boys.

M.     *Bene! Tu surge! Quid facis?*
P.      *Surgo.*
M.     *Quid facit ille?*
Class.   *Surgit.*

         Then a boy is given a ruler and told in English to walk about the class, tell different boys to rise and ask them what they are doing. Thus we get:

P[1].     *Surge! Quid facis?*
P[2].     *Surgo.*
P[1].     *Quid facit ille?*
Class.   *Surgit.*

         This is repeated for several boys.

         Then the master pointing at himself says *Ego sum magister,* and pointing at a boy says *Tu es puer.*

         Then pointing at another boy he says *Ille est puer.*

|        |                                                                                                                                                                                                                 |
| ------ | --------------------------------------------------------------------------------------------------------------------------------------------------------------------------------------------------------------- |
|        | This is repeated; then the *'surgo'* business is gone through again with several questions such as *Quid facio? Quid facis?* thus preparing the way for                                                         |
| M.     | *Ego sum magister. Tu es puer. Ego sum magister. Quis sum?**                                                                                                                                                    |
| P.     | *Magister es.*                                                                                                                                                                                                  |
| M.     | *Ille est puer. Quis est ille?*                                                                                                                                                                                 |
| P.     | *Puer est ille.*                                                                                                                                                                                                |
| M.     | *Ego sum magister, non sum puer. Sumne puer?* The *ne* is not yet, of course, understood.                                                                                                                       |
| P.     | *Non.* This need not necessarily be objected to at first; later on, *minime* may be substituted.                                                                                                                |
| M.     | *Quis sum?*                                                                                                                                                                                                     |
| P.     | *Magister es.*                                                                                                                                                                                                  |
| M.     | [pointing to a boy] *Estne ille magister?*                                                                                                                                                                      |
| P.     | *Non, ille est puer.*                                                                                                                                                                                           |
| M.     | *Sumne ego magister?* No reply is forthcoming because the Latin for 'yes' is not known, so the master proceeds himself:                                                                                         |
| M.     | *Ita. Ego sum magister. Estne ille puer?*                                                                                                                                                                       |
| P.     | *Ita. Ille est puer.*                                                                                                                                                                                           |
|        | The master then says to a boy, whom he takes out as before, but now speaking in Latin *Tu es magister, ego sum puer. Dic 'Surge' et 'Quid facio?' et 'Quid facis?'* One of the brightest boys must, of course, be chosen at first. He will walk about the room, and questions and answers such as the following will be made: |
| P¹.    | *Surge! Quid facis?*                                                                                                                                                                                            |
| P².    | *Surgo.*                                                                                                                                                                                                        |
| P¹.    | *Quid facit ille?*                                                                                                                                                                                              |
| Class. | *Ille surgit.*                                                                                                                                                                                                  |
| P¹.    | *Estne ille magister?*                                                                                                                                                                                          |
| Class. | *Non, ille est puer.*                                                                                                                                                                                           |

\* The master should speak very clearly, very slowly and very deliberately. If he does so, few boys will fail to pick up, for example, the *es* or *est* required in the following answers.

And so on. If the boy-master makes a mistake, such as the omission of the *ne* in *Estne ille magister?* it is easy for the real master to prompt him.

N.B.—That different boys shall thus take the part of master from the very earliest lessons is a point of extreme importance. Those who have not tried it can have no idea of the difference it makes both to accuracy and interest.

## § 3.

No English at all is spoken in this lesson until two minutes before the end when the homework is set. Henceforth it is to be understood that no English is spoken either by master or boys, unless the contrary is expressly stated.

- Revision of previous lesson.
- The plural of *surgo* and of *sum*.

| | |
|---|---|
| *M.* | [placing a second chair next to his own on the rostrum] Beckons a boy and says *Veni huc,* then *Sede,* and motions him down. The boy sits on the chair next to the master, who says to him *Surge*. The master rises simultaneously with the boy, and addressing the class says, *Surgimus.* |
| | This is repeated; then the master asks the class, *Quid facimus?* No answer is, of course, given, because the second person plural is not known, so the master prompts—*Surgitis*. Then again, *Nos surgimus. Quid facimus?* |
| *Class:* | *Surgitis.* |
| *M.* | [addressing P¹ in class] *Surge!* [and to P²] *Tu quoque surge!* As they rise the master says *Vos surgitis*. This is repeated with the other boys. Then the master and then boy-master rise saying, *Nos surgimus. Quid facimus?* |
| *Class:* | *Vos surgitis.* |
| | The master, as before, tells two boys to rise and addressing the boy-master says, *Illi surgunt*. He repeats this with other boys and then asks the boy-master *Quid faciunt illi?* |
| *Pᵐ.* | *Illi surgunt.* [Pᵐ is the boy-master.] |
| *M.* | Repeat *Ego sum magister, tu es puer* etc. Then addressing Pᵐ: *Ego sum magister et tu es magister: nos sumus magistri.* |
| | Then pointing to two boys, *Tu es puer et tu es puer; vos estis pueri.* |
| | *Nos sumus magistri, vos estis pueri. Qui sumus nos?* |

| | |
|---|---|
| Class: | Vos estis magistri. |
| M. | Bene. Nos sumus magistri; vos estis pueri. Then addressing P$^m$: *Nos sumus magistri; illi sunt pueri. Qui sumus nos?* |
| P$^m$. | Nos sumus magistri. |
| M. | Bene. Nos sumus magistri; illi sunt pueri. Qui sunt illi? |
| P$^m$. | Illi sunt pueri. |
| M. | Bene. Nos sumus magistri, illi sunt pueri. Then addressing the class, *Qui estis vos?* |
| Class. | Pueri sumus. |
| M. | Bene. Pueri estis. Qui sumus nos? |
| Class. | Vos estis magistri. |
| M. | Bene. Nos sumus magistri. Then addressing P$^m$, but pointing to the class, *Illi sunt pueri*. This iterative style is, of course, deliberate; it is thus that the class is able to pick up the new forms. The master then takes chalk, and, writing on the board *Nos sumus magistri* asks *Quid facio?* No response, of course, is given, and so the master prompts *Scribo*. He then gives the chalk to P$^m$ and says *Scribe 'Illi sunt pueri.' Quid facis?* |
| P$^m$. | Scribo. |
| M. | Ita. Scribis. Ego scribo et tu scribis. Then pointing to P$^m$, but addressing a boy in the class, *Quid facit ille?* |
| P. | Ille scribit. |
| M. | Bene. Ille scribit.

The master then writes out the whole tense on the board thus: |

| | |
|---|---|
| Ego surgo | ego sum magister |
| tu surgis | tu es magister |
| ille surgit | ille est magister |
| nos surgimus | nos sumus magistri |
| vos surgitis | vos estis magistri |
| illi surgunt | illi sunt magistri |

| | |
|---|---|
| M. | As he starts to write, the master addresses the class and says *Scribite vos*, and all write it out in |

their notebooks. [Each boy has an notebook in order to write down anything necessary.] Then the master proceeds *Ego sum magister. Quid est haec?* [taking up the chalk] *Haec est creta.* Then, laying it down and taking it up again, *Quid facio? Cretam capio et scribo.* Then, handing it to a boy *Cape cretam et scribe 'creta.'*
*Quid facis?*

| | |
|---|---|
| P. | *Capio cretam.* |
| M. | *Bene. Cretam capis. Quid facit ille?* |
| Class. | *Cretam capit.* |
| M. | *Bene. Cretam capit et scribit. Tu, cape cretam et scribe 'capio.' Quid facis?* |
| P. | *Capio cretam et scribo.* |
| M. | *Bene. Cretam capis et scribis. Tu, Palinure, cape cretam. Tu es Palinurus. Nomen tibi est Palinurus.* [This was vaguely understood to mean 'Your name is Palinurus.'] *Quid tibi est nomen?* |
| P. | *Palinurus.* |
| M. | *Dic 'Nomen mihi est Palinurus.'* |
| P. | *Nomen mihi est Palinurus.* |

Names were thus given to four or five of the sharper boys, and they were asked in turn *Quid est tibi nomen?* and made to say *Nomen mihi est Urbanus, Viator,* etc. The master then looked round at their writing-out of the present of *surgo* and *sum,* and, finding their English names on their notebooks, exclaimed *Quid est hoc? Scribe 'Viator,' 'Urbanus,'* etc., as the case might be. All who had acquired Latin names proceeded to scratch out their English ones and to substitute their newly acquired Latin ones. In naming the boys it is well to keep to real praenomina such as *Marcus, Quintus, Decimus, Sextus, Titus,* etc., or to appropriate renderings of the English surnames such as *Faber, Muscus, Lupus,* etc.

For homework the class was told to learn the two tenses which they had written out.

## § 4.

- Revision of previous work.

M.     *Do tibi cretam. Da mihi cretam. Quid facis?*
P.      *Do tibi cretam.*
M.     *Quid mihi das?*
P.      *Cretam tibi do.*
M.     *Bene. Cretam mihi das.* Then, addressing the class but indicating the boy—*Quid facit ille?* and, prompting, *Dat mihi cretam.* Action and question are repeated, and now the class can reply.
Class.   *Cretam tibi dat.*

       Now the master calls out a boy and striking him, says *Pulso te. Pulsa me.* As the boy does so the master asks, *Quid facis?*

P.      *Pulso te.*
M.     *Bene. Pulsas me.* Then to the class, *Ille me pulsat. Quid facit ille?*
Class.   *Pulsat te.*
M.     *Quem pulsat?*
Class.   *Te pulsat.* The order of words is important and should be practised from the beginning; great scope is given for this in the seventh or eighth and, of course, in all subsequent, lessons.

       *Do, das, dat* and *Pulso, pulsas, pulsat* are then revised with different boys.

M.     **[the master places the chalk upon the table]** *Creta est in mensa; in mensa est creta. Ubi est creta?*
P.      *In mensa est creta.*
M.     *Bene respondes. Cretam tibi do. Quid facio?*
P.      *Cretam mihi das.* This is repeated with different boys.

       Then the master explains: *In sententia 'Creta est in mensa,' 'creta' est subiectum sententiae, casus est nominativus.*

       *In sententia 'Cretam tibi do,' 'cretam' est obiectum verbi 'do', casus est accusativus.* Then on the board is written:

|  |  |  |  |
|---|---|---|---|
| *Nominativus casus.* | CretA | ego | tu |
| *Accusitavus casus.* | CretAM | me | te |
| *Dativus casus.* |  | mihi | tibi |

This is written out by all in their notebooks and learnt as homework. It serves to draw attention to three different cases as such. These particular words are chosen because they have all been correctly *used* and understood by the class already. This lesson should contain plenty of revision.

## § 5.

- Practice and revision of previous work.

The master begins by writing on the board:

|   |   |   |
|---|---|---|
| *Nom.* | *CretA* | *UrbanUS* |
| *Acc.* | *CretAM* | *UrbanUM* |

M. *Urbane, pulsa Palinurum! Quid facis?*
P. *Pulso Palinurus.*
M. *Minime. Pulsas Palinurum.*
   This is repeated and the correct answer is obtained.
M. *Palinure, pulsa Urbanum! Quid facis?*
P. *Pulso Urbanum.*
M. *Quid facit Palinurus?*
Class. *Ille pulsat Urbanum.*

This is practised with six or seven pairs of boys. Then the master writes on the board:

A. *Palinurum pulsat Urbanus.*
B. *Urbanum pulsat Palinurus.*

and pointing to (A) asks *Quis pulsat?*
Class. *Urbanus pulsat.*
M. *Bene. Quem pulsat Urbanus.*

The same is done with (B). Similar practice may be made with

A. *Palinurum pulsat Urbanus.*
B. *Palinurus pulsat Urbanum.*

Even the dullest boy cannot help seeing the importance of the endings in such sentences. More names are now given to the boys, and there follows practice of *'Nomen est mihi,'* etc. Then a boy is made master, and he practises the *'pulsa'* business, telling different boys to strike their neighbours, asking each boy what he is doing, and then asking the class what the boy is doing.

The master introduces *'aperio ianuam'* and writes out the present indicative of the four regular conjugations on the board. *Sedeo* had been used already, although the attention of the class had not been drawn to it.

| I | II | III | IV |
|---|----|-----|-----|
| *pulso* | *sedeo* | *surgo* | *aperio* |
| *pulsas* | *sedes* | *surgis* | *aperis* |
| *pulsat* | *sedet* | *surgit* | *aperit* |
| *pulsamus* | *sedemus* | *surgimus* | *aperimus* |
| *pulsatis* | *sedetis* | *surgitis* | *aperitis* |
| *pulsant* | *sedent* | *surgunt* | *aperiunt* |

This is set to be learnt as homework.

## § 6.

- Practice of present indicative of the four regular conjugations.

Then:

| | |
|---|---|
| M. | *Da mihi cretam. Quid facis?* |
| P. | *Do tibi cretam.* |
| M. | *Urbanum pulsa, Palinure! Quid facis?* |
| P. | *Pulso Urbanum.* |
| M. | [to class] *Urbanum quis pulsat?* |
| Class. | *Palinurus Urbanum pulsat.* |
| M. | *Palinurum pulsa, Urbane! Quid facis?* |
| P. | *Pulso Palinurum.* |
| M. | *Palinurum quis pulsat?* |
| Class. | *Palinurum Urbanus pulsat.* |

So with 'Marcum pulsa,' etc.

| | |
|---|---|
| M. | [touching boy] *Te tango. Quid facio?* |
| P. | *Me tangis.* |
| M. | *Tange Decimum. Quid facis?* |
| P. | *Tango Decimum.* |
| M. | [to class] *Quid facit ille?* |
| Class. | *Ille tangit Decimum.* And so on; then |
| M. | [giving notebook to boy] *Hic est libellus. Libellum tibi do. Quid tibi do?* |
| P. | *Libellum mihi das.* |

This is repeated with other boys, then the master gives a pile of notebooks to a boy and says: *Tu distribue. Da libellum, et dic 'Libellum tibi do; quid facio?'* This boy gives the books round to the whole class and goes through the formula with each boy. The master, addressing this boy upon another boy's reply, says *Dic, 'Bene,' magister!* Thus we get:

| | |
|---|---|
| P$^m$. | *Libellum tibi do. Quid facio?* |
| P. | *Libellum mihi das.* |
| P$^m$. | *Bene.* |

When a wrong answer came, he was told to say, *Male, non bene.*

         The master, noticing the absence of a certain boy, says: *Nanus abest. Ubi est Nanus?* As he speaks the master points to the place usually occupied by the boy in question.

M.     *Quis abest?*
Class.  *Nanus abest.*
M.     *Et Dux abest. Nanus et Dux ab...* [pause]
Class.                                        *-sunt.*

        Practise with other verbs such as *Marcus et Decimus sedent, Quintus et Manlius ambulant,* etc.

## § 7.

- Revision as usual.

| | |
|---|---|
| M. | *Abestne Nanus?* |
| Class. | *Non abest.* |
| M. | *Quis abest?* [prompting] *Nemo abest. Quis abest?* |
| Class. | *Nemo abest.* |
| M. | *Hic est digitus. Quid est?* |
| Class. | *Digitus est.* |
| M. | *Digitum tango. Quid tango?* |
| Class. | *Digitum tangis.* |
| | So with *oculus, nasus, capillus.* |
| M. | *Hic est digitus; magistri est digitus, non est digitus Urbani. Cuius est digitus? Magistri est digitus. Hic est oculus. Magistri est oculus. Cuius est oculus?* |
| Class. | *Magistri est oculus. Cuius* is not, of course, known as the genitive of *quis,* but it is understood, as the answer proves. |
| M. | *Estne hic digitus Urbani?* |
| Class. | *Non, magistri est digitus.* |
| M. | *Capillum Nani tango. Quid tango?* |
| Class. | *Capillum Nani tangis.* |
| M. | *Cuius capillum tango?* |
| Class. | *Nani capillum tangis.* So with *oculus* and *nasus.* |
| M. | *Palinure, tange capillum Bruti. Quid facis?* |
| P. | *Tango capillum Bruti.* |
| M. | *Quid facit Palinurus?* |
| Class. | *Tangit capillum Bruti.* |
| M. | *Cuius capillum tangit?* |
| Class. | *Bruti capillum tangit.* |
| M. | *Hic est nasus; cuius est nasus?* |
| Class. | *Magistri est nasus.* |
| M. | *Estne hic Sexti nasus?* |
| Class. | *Non, Nani est nasus.* |
| M. | *Dicite 'Minime; Nani est nasus.'* |
| Class. | *Minime; Nani est nasus.* |
| M. | *Da mihi libellum. Quid facis?* |
| P. | *Do tibi libellum.* |

| | |
|---|---|
| M. | *Cuius est libellus?* |
| Class. | *Decimi est libellus.* |
| M. | *Palinure, libellum Urbani cape et mihi da. Quid facis?* |
| P. | *Libellum Urbani capio et tibi do.* |

This is repeated with different boys. The master then writes up on the board:

| | |
|---|---|
| Nom. | *libellus* |
| Voc. | *libelle* |
| Acc. | *libellum* |
| Gen. | *libelli* |

## § 8.

- Revision as usual. Then:

| | |
|---|---|
| M. | *Palinure, cape libellum Nani et mihi da. Quid facis?* |
| P. | *Libellum Nani capio et tibi do.* |
| M. | *Libellum Nani Urbano da.* |
| P. | *Libellum Nani Urbano do.* |
| M. | *Quid facit Palinurus?* |
| Class. | *Libellum Nani Urbano dat.* |
| M. | *Decime, cape libellum Sexti et Indico da. Quid facis?* |
| P. | *Libellum Sexti capio et Indico do.* |
| M. | *Quid facit Decimus?* |
| Class. | *Libellum Sexti capit et Indico dat.* |
| M. | *Quinte, libellum Sexti cape at Sexto da. Quid facis?* [At this moment Indicus, of course, is in possession of the book.] |
| P. | *Libellum Sexti capio at Sexto do.* |
| M. | *Quid facit Quintus?* |
| Class. | *Libellum Sexti capit et Sexto dat.* |

And so on with other boys. Then:

| | |
|---|---|
| M. | [touching boy's hair] *Quid facio?* |
| Class. | *Capillum Urbani tangis.* |
| M. | *Bene. Capillum Urbani digito tango. Quo instrumento capillum Urbani tangi? Digito capillum tango. Quo instrumento te tango?* |
| P. | *Digito me tangis.* |
| M. | *Digito Nanum tange. Quid facis?* |
| P. | *Digito Nanum tango.* |
| M. | *Capillum Quinti digito tange. Quid facis?* |
| P. | *Capillum Quinti digito tango.* |

Then '*Quid facit ille*' etc.

| | |
|---|---|
| M. | *Hic est calamus. Calamo scribimus. Quid facimus calamo?* |
| Class. | *Scribimus calamo.* |
| M. | *Quo instrumento scribimus?* |
| Class. | *Calamo scribimus.* |

M. Scribite calamo in libellis:
| | |
|---|---|
| Nom. | libellus |
| Voc. | libelle |
| Acc. | libellum |
| Gen. | libelli |
| Dat. | libello |
| Abl. | libello |

This lesson should contain plenty of revision.

## § 9.

| | |
|---|---|
| M. | Te specto. Urbanum specto. Palinurum specto. Quid facio? |
| Class. | Nanum spectas. |
| M. | Sextum digito demonstro. Decimum digito demonstro. Quid facio? |
| Class. | Decimum digito demonstras. |
| M. | Haec est ferula. Hoc est pulpitum. Ferulam capio et puliptum ascendo. Quid facio? |
| Class. | Ferulam capis et pulpitum ascendas. |
| M. | Male respondetis. Est ascendo, ascendis, ascendit. Est tertiae coniugationis. Spectate libellos; primae coniugationis est pulso, secundae est sedeo, tertiae est surgo, quartae est aperio. Et ascendo declinatur ut surgo. Ferulam capio et pulpitum ascendo. Quid facio? |
| Class. | Ferulam capis et pulpitum ascendis. |
| M. | Bene. Nunc, Viator, tu cape ferulam et pulpitum ascende. Quid facis? |
| P. | Capio ferulam at pulpitum ascendo. |
| M. | Ianuam aperio. Quid facio? |
| Class. | Aperis ianuam. |
| M. | Ianuam claudo. Quid facio? |
| Class. | Ianuam claudis. |
| M. | Tu, Sexte, ianuam claude. |
| P. | Ianuam claudo. |
| M. | [addressing boy on rostrum] Tu, Viator, ferula Sextum demonstra, Sextum specta et dic 'Ianuam claudis.' |
| $P^1$. | Ianuam claudis. |
| M. | Tu, Quinte, ferulam cape et pulpitum ascende. |
| $P^2$. | Ferulam capio et pulpitum ascendo. |
| $P^1$. | Ferula capis et pulpitum ascendis. |
| M. | Tu, Nane, libellum Decimi cape. |
| P. | Libellum Decimi capio. |
| $P^1$. | [at a nod from the master] Libellum Decimi capis. |
| M. | [addressing $P^2$] Tu, Quinte, ferula Nanum demonstra, sed pueros specta, et dic 'Libellum Decimi capit.' |
| $P^2$. | Libellum Decimi capit. |
| M. | Urbane, libellum Palinuri cape et Tauro da. |

| | |
|---|---|
| P. | *Libellum Palinuri capio et Tauro do.* |
| P¹. | *Libellum Palinuri capis et Tauro das.* |
| P². | *Libellum Palinuri capit et Tauro dat.* |

So on with other boys and sentences, the two boys on the rostrum always acting as chorus. Then the two chorus-boys are changed thus:

| | |
|---|---|
| M. | *Tu, Viator, nunc descende et ferulam Tauro da.* |
| P¹. | *Ego descendo et ferulam Tauro do.* |
| P². | *Ille descendit et ferulam Tauro dat.* |
| M. | *Tu, Taure, pulpitum ascende.* [Taurus is now the new P¹.] |
| P¹. | *Pulpitum ascendo.* |
| P². | *Pulpitum ascendit.* |
| M. | [addressing P²] *Et tu, Quinte, nunc descende et ferulam Decimo da.* |
| P². | *Ego descendo et ferulam Decimo do.* |
| P¹. | [at a nod from the master] *Tu descendis et ferulam Decimo das.* |
| M. | *Tu, Decime, pulpitum ascende.* [Decimus is now the new P².] |
| P². | *Pulpitum ascendo.* |
| M. | *Antoni, libellum Manlio da.* |
| P. | *Libellum Manlio da.* |
| P¹. | *Libellum Manlio das.* |
| P². | *Libellum Manlio dat.* |

And so on with other sentences and boys, making frequent changes of chorus-boys.

## § 10.

At this point it was discovered that the difference between the Subject and the Object of a sentence had not been fully grasped by the weaker members of the class, and so for the first quarter of an hour of this lesson a grammatical explanation was given in English of the 'Subject-Predicate-Direct Object' relation, and the difference between such sentences as,

*Palinurus Urbanum pulsat*
and, *Palinurum Urbanus pulsat*

was once more insisted upon. The rest of the lesson was taken up by the writing of words (all so far used) by different boys on the board, in order to make sure that they could correctly write them. Each boy copied down all these words in his notebook. This latter portion of the lesson, was, of course, conducted in Latin.

## § 11.

- Nom., Acc. and Gen. plural of Second Declension.

It does not seem necessary to give a verbatim report of this and the following lessons. The method is the same as before, e.g.:

| | |
|---|---|
| M. | Hi sunt lebelli. Libellos capio. Quid capio? |
| Class. | Libellos capis. |
| M. | Hi sunt oculi. Quid facio? [shutting his eyes] |
| Class. | Oculos claudis. |
| M. | Quid nunc facio? |
| Class. | Oculos aperis. |
| M. | Hi sunt pueri. Hi sunt libelli. Libelli puerorum sunt. Quorum sunt libelli? |
| Class. | Puerorum sunt libelli. |
| M. | Puerorum libellos capio. Quid facio? |
| Class. | Puerorum libellos capis. |

Plenty of practice. New cases set for homework.

## § 12.

- A thorough revision of § 11. Then:

| | |
|---|---|
| M. | *Hic est liber. Parvus est liber. Hic est liber. Magnus est liber. Qualis est hic liber?* |
| Class. | *Magnus est liber.* |
| M. | *Qualis est hic liber?* |
| Class. | *Parvus est liber.* |
| M. | *Librum magnum tollo. Quid facio?* |
| Class. | *Librum magnum tollis.* |

It should be understood that whenever a mistake is made, as, for example, *tollas* here for *tollis*, the master corrects in the manner indicated in § 9. Thus, the class becomes familiar with such grammatical terms as *coniugatio* and *declinatio*.

| | |
|---|---|
| M. | *Librum magni pueri capio et parvo puero do. Quid facio?* |
| Class. | *Librum magni pueri capis et parvo puero das.* |

Practise this also with the chorus-boys as in § 9.

| | |
|---|---|
| M. | *Creta est alba. Qualis est creta?* |
| Class. | *Alba est creta.* |
| M. | *Estne pulpitum album.* |
| Class. | *Minime. Creta est alba; pulpitum non est album.* |

And so on with different coloured books, etc. The singular of parvus is now written out and learnt as homework.

## § 13.

At this stage, and not before, the master puts *Initium* into the hands of his class. It will be observed that the boys know:

1. The present indicative of the four regular conjugations, including words like *capio* and *facio*. It is not necessary to treat these as a special type. Get the class to judge the conjugation of a verb from the infinitive (the form is readily understood), and always give the infinitive of every new verb.
2. The present indicative of *sum*.
3. A second declension masculine word such as *libellus*.
4. The singular of *parvus* and, by implication, the singular of words such as *creta* and *rostrum*.
5. The nom., acc., and dat. of pronouns of the first and second persons.
6. Certain isolated words such as *quis, quid, cuius, quorum, qualis,* etc.
7. A certain number of nouns represented by classroom objects (*ianua*, etc.), parts of the body (*nasus*, etc.), and several verbs easily explained by performing the actions (*ascendo*, etc.).
8. A few adjectives also explained by demonstration (*parvus, magnus, albus,* etc.).
9. A few adverbs (*bene, male,* etc.).
10. A few forms of pronouns (*hic, hi, ille,* etc.).

In *Initium* any new grammatical forms which occur in any section are printed at the end of the section for convenience of reference. A compendium of the whole of the grammar is also printed at the back of the book for purposes of revision. As to vocabulary, we have proceeded on the following principles:

A. Anything which has occurred in the first twelve sections of this *libellus* is assumed as known, though the words are inserted (without any

explanation) for the sake of giving their declension, gender, or conjugation.
B. Any verb, the meaning of which can readily be explained by action is given in the vocabulary (without any comment) for the sake of its grammatical formation, etc.
C. A few words have English equivalents attached, e.g. *potius* = rather.

Personally, we prefer that the boys should not have a printed vocabulary, but that all new words should be explained by the teacher, written on the blackboard by some boy and copied down by all into their notebooks. Nouns must always have their genitive singular and gender attached, thus: *ped, pedis* (m.). This makes it unnecessary to learn more than one type for the third declension. [Neuters and gen. pl. in *-ium* are of course specially commented upon.] As soon as the perfect indicative has been learnt all verbs must be written up with the infinitive and perfect attached, thus: *Surgō, -ere, surrēxī*.

Nevertheless we have printed a vocabulary as a concession to others. It has been perforated in order that it may be torn out by those teachers who do not wish to have it. Perhaps it may be useful as an aid to ready paraphrasing. But certain words, such as *licet, oportet,* cannot be explained by a Latin paraphrase, but are readily explained *in their context* during the conduct of a class. As the meanings of such words are assumed in the vocabulary it may be well to indicate here the manner in which they are made intelligible to the class.

**Licet.** A boy makes a mistake in writing on the board and another boy enthusiastically waves his hand in obvious desire to correct it. Then the master says, *Licet tibi corrigere*. Later on a similar instance occurs and the master before allowing the boy to go up to the board says to him, *Dic 'Licetne mihi corrigere?'* Whereupon the boy says it, and the master adds, *Licet tibi corrigere*. After a few repitions this becomes familiar to all, in fact *Licetne mihi?* is one of the commonest phrases on the lips of the class.

**Oportet.** Similarly when a mistake is made orally, the master says, *Non bene dicis. Oportet te dicere....* Then, when he has used the phrase once or twice, he will upon a similar occasion ask a second boy, *Quid oportet Marcum dicere, Quinte?* etc. He will also vary this, at a somewhat later stage, by the gerund *dicendum est, recitandum est,* etc.

**Volo** is also most readily explained in context, e.g. *Libellum mihi monstra. Ego volo videre,* or, upon offering something to a boy, *Visne habere?* Very soon *Quid dicere volt?* becomes quite a common question to the class whenever a boy hesitates about anything. Of course these irregular verbs (*volo, fero, eo,* etc.) are all learnt by heart after, but not before, the necessity of using them has occurred.

## § 14.

### The Grammar.

The new grammar is taken up in sections; the chief forms which are required for any particular section are printed at the end of that section, so that, after the section has been read through, that amount of grammar may be practised in class or learnt as homework. A compendium of the whole grammar is printed, for convenience of reference, at the end of the book, and it is here only that all grammatical forms not peculiarly connected with any particular section will be found. This applies to such things as the present indicative of *volo, possum,* etc., the numerals, and other things which will be introduced and explained in quite an incidental way at first; then later—as soon as they come to be frequently required, and should therefore be part of the possession of the class—they will definitely be 'turned up' at the back of the book and learnt as homework. The third declension is treated as one; in future the boys will always take down such words with the genitive singular and gender added. An additional example of a neuter noun is, of course, given; but the first year is not the time to worry the pupil with the ablative singular in *-ī* or *-e;* even the genitive plural in *-ium* will only be mentioned as the need occurs. The teacher may, if he pleases, give the rough rule about non-increasing nouns, without, of course, dealing with exceptions.

It will be noticed that almost all the common pronouns (*is, hic, ille, qui, ipse, alius, alter, idem*) are grouped together at the end of one section. This is done deliberately, as it has been found that the similarity of their declension enables them all to be quickly grasped by the learner.

The method of introducing new tenses calls for a word of explanation. A little piece of oral work should certainly preface the section which introduces the new forms. For example, the perfect tense should be introduced to the class somewhat after the following fashion: The master performs certain simple actions asking the class what he is doing; suppose the replies to be *Cretam capis; In tabula nigra scribis.*

The master then sits down and asks *Quid nunc facio?* He gets the answer *Sedes,* and proceeds himself, *Quid antea feci? Cretam cepi, deinde in tabula nigra scripsi et nunc sedeo. Nunc sedeo, cretam non capio, neque in tabula scribo. Sed cretam antea cepi, et in tabula scripsi. Nunc autem sedeo. 'Sedeo'* est praesens tempus. *'Scripsi'* est perfectum.

The master will then perform some more simple actions such as walking about, opening and shutting the door or a window, and will then make the class reply not only to the question *Quid facio?* but also to *Quid feci?* Then a boy will be told to go through similar actions and ask similar questions. The whole of one lesson should be devoted to this preliminary oral work before the class reads the section which contains the new tense. Some ten verbs will probably have been employed, and all will be written on the board and copied by the class into their notebooks, like this:

*scrībō, scrībere, scrīpsī*
*aperiō, aperīre, aperuī*
etc., etc.

Probably before the end of the lesson is reached most of the new endings will have been practised, and the endings of all persons may then be written down and learnt. Thus:

| | |
|---|---|
| *Prīma persōna* | -ī |
| *Secunda persōna* | -istī |
| *Tertia persōna* | -it |
| *Pluraliter* | |
| *Prīma persōna* | -imus |
| *Secunda persōna* | -istis |
| *Tertia persōna* | -ērunt |

The class is now in a position to proceed with the reading of the book.

The method of introducing the future tense will be similar. The master while seated says, let us suppose, *Spectate me, discipuli. Ego nunc sedeo, sed mox surgam et Marcum pulsabo.* He thereupon rises and approaches Marcus who will be dull indeed if he does not anticipate what is coming. The master continues, *Nunc Marcum pulso, sed mox iterum sedebo,* and so on with other simple actions. Then, as before, various boys will be made to perform, and the whole procedure will be similar to that which introduced the perfect tense, the difference being that there are two entirely different sets of endings to be mastered. If the teacher think fit he may devote the lesson following this to practising the present, future, and perfect all together instead of at once proceeding to continue reading from the book. Similar practice will, of course, precede the sections which introduce the imperfect, pluperfect, and future perfect respectively.

## § 15.

The book is not meant to be used by the class without the help of the teacher. We assume that he will always be ready to make any necessary explanation by demonstrating on the blackboard or by other suitable means. Thus after using other tenses such as the future and the perfect the points of time may be indicated by a line drawn upon the board. Take, for example, this short piece of narrative:

*Puer ad flumen iit; nunc in ripa stat; mox natabit.*

This may be expressed graphically thus:

*Tempus perfectum* → *Tempus praesens* → *Tempus futurum*
*Puer ad flumen iit*　　*In ripa stat*　　　　*Mox natabit*

The teacher who can draw will, of course, add little illustrations under each tense.

We give one more example of the kind of explanation which we leave in the hands of the teacher. In the little piece of dialogue entitled *Salutator* occur the expressions *prima* and *secunda hora*. In order to explain Roman time the teacher will draw a circle on the board, and beginning at the point representing six o'clock in English time, will point out, in Latin of course, that the period from that point to the point representing seven o'clock in English time is in Latin *prima hora*. He will fill out the whole dial and the boys will copy it down in their notebooks.

Perhaps an example of this sort of explanation with more advanced boys may be useful. While the fourth form was reading the second Aeneid the words *Si omnes uno ordine habetis Achivos* were paraphrased by a boy as *Si putatis omnes Graecos similes esse*. All understood this paraphrase but some did not understand how it was that the two phrases were equivalent. Therefore the master after getting a boy to explain *Te pro hoste habeo* as *Puto te esse hostem*, wrote the following upon the board:

*Discipuli*

| Abominandi | Non ita mali | Boni |
|---|---|---|
| Marcus<br>Quintus<br>Sextus<br>Decimus | Ceteri | Nemo |

And then said *Marcum, Quintum, Sextum, Decimum in eodem ordine habeo. Puto eos similes esse.* Thus all understood how the phrase came to have this meaning. A good teacher will readily perceive whenever such explanatory demonstration is necessary, and we leave him to his own resources to supply it. We should like to add that it is only by such means as these that teaching upon the direct method can be freed from the reproach of inculcating vague impressions instead of clean understanding.

## § 16.
### The Plays.

There are in the book, in addition to obviously dramatic dialogues such as *Mercurius,* four short plays (*Iulii exitium, Salutator, Ludus,* and *Mancipiorum auctio*) together with a somewhat longer one entitled *Puer qui a ludo se abstinuit.* This latter is placed at the end of the book, but it may be read as soon as the class is familiar with the fifth declension and the imperfect tense, i.e. just before it comes to *The House that Jack built.* With this exception the rest of the matter in the book is arranged in the order in which it should be read.

We consider the use of such plays one of the most vital aids to successful teaching on the direct method. No teacher who has tried such work will have any doubts about the added interest which it provides; it has also for our purpose a more specific psychological purpose. It helps to make Latin more real to the learner. This is true even when the subject is not really a Roman one; in fact, for young children, it is perhaps more true in such a case. An example will make our meaning clear: the little episode in *Mancipiorum auctio* where a purchaser buys the tightrope walker to play with his children is *more real* to a child than the murder of Caesar in *Iulii exitium,* for example, simply because it is, as the logicians would say, more within his 'sphere of discourse.' And it is a principle of the direct method to make Latin a living and not a dead thing to the learner. Few will feel that Latin is debased by being applied to such things as this; if anyone does feel so, we can only assure him that our experience has taught us that the reading of such frivolous trifles by a child of twelve or thirteen by no means spoils his appreciation of the real dignity and grandeur of Latin literature in later years.

The plays must, of course, be acted, and the utmost freedom should be given. Our boys, for example, when acting the *Puer qui a ludo se abstinuit* make 'bad eggs' by screwing up pieces of paper which are hurled all over the classroom to repeated lusty cries of *Io triumphe!* at the hapless Britons.

If the master has the right hold over his class—that perfect discipline which is not incompatible with perfect freedom—a single tap from his ruler upon a desk or form will produce immediate stillness and silence, so that he may make any necessary correction or other remark. If the class has been well trained such interruptions will not be frequent. Perhaps it is best to read the play through first as an ordinary piece of narrative; otherwise the continual stoppages for writing new words down in the notebooks are apt to become irksome. But once the words have become understood the play should be acted with book in hand; nor will it be acted only once. Perhaps parts will be learnt at home, and so the play becomes part of the 'stock-in-trade' of the class; in either case it will be revived from time to time either with or without books. Many boys will learn more from acting these little plays than from any other part of their work.

## § 17.
### The Exercises.

But acting plays does not produce linguistic accuracy. The boy who is best in a play may well be an unholy terror at an exercise. Neither side must be neglected, so the master will pay most attention to the side which the boys are most naturally inclined to neglect. He may, if necessary, refuse to allot a part in acting the plays to any boy who is not doing well at the 'formal' side of the work, at least until he notices an effort to improve. There are only about twenty exercises in the whole of the book, and it is suggested that these should be the only written work done during the first year. *They are not part of the teaching,* but are to be used as a check upon inaccuracy or as a test of knowledge gained. If the teacher finds that the majority of his class cannot do them without a single mistake, then he will know that his teaching has been inadequate. He will then, not give his class more exercises (which is the first, and wrong, impulse), but concentrate more attention upon the formal aspect of the oral work. It is the oral work, especially in the first year, which does the teaching; in fact the exercises are not for the sake of the boys at all. They are a means of informing the teacher whether he has been doing his work properly or not.

## § 18.

### Incidentals.

The more experienced the teacher upon the direct method becomes, the more he will find that he can teach incidentally. In fact we question whether the direct method can be a success in the hands of one who will not avail himself of the countless opportunities which occur of teaching something about Roman habits or Latin idiom in connection with one's daily converse with a class. The scope is infinite: a boy sneezes—not only is *sternuo* taught, but also *salvus sis!*; a boy blows his nose—not only is *emungo* taught, but also *emunctae naris homo*. A single word will often open up quite a large 'sphere of discourse'; the word *currus*, for example, brings in *auriga, quadrigae, bigae, rota, flagellum, meta,* etc. For this purpose it is necessary to have at hand plenty of wall pictures and other illustrations; Cybulski's series of *Tabulae quibus antiquitates Romanae et Graecae illustrantur* are most useful. One can also manage to get little models of a *circus, ballista,* etc. Excursuses such as these, however, must be left entirely to the initiative of the teacher. But much grammar, too, may be taught in this incidental way, and, as this method is assumed in the arrangement of *Initium*, a word or two of explanation must be given here. In the very first section occurs *nobiscum*. The class does not know this form, but it knows *nos*. The master therefore says, "*Nobis est casus ablativus; 'nobiscum' significat 'cum nobis'; ita enim dicunt Romani—nobiscum, vobiscum, mecum, tecum.*" The personal pronouns are printed in full at the end of the book; these may be referred to if desired.

## § 19.

We give here a specimen of the method of conducting the reading of a somewhat more advanced portion of the book. Let us suppose that the class has just reached the section about *The House that Jack built*. The boys are too young to have any explanation of Latin metre given to them, but by the end of the piece they will have obtained some feeling for the rhythm of the lines and they will not find much difficulty in committing the whole to memory. A boy stands up and reads:

P.     *Aspicis hic aedes quas aedificavit Iacchus.*
          Then:
          *Non intellego 'aspicis.'*
P[2].   *Vides.*
M.    *Scribite partes principales: aspicio, -ere, aspexi, aspectum.*
          *Aedes* will be understood from the picture, but the master will give *domus* and *villa* as synonyms.
P.     *Quid significat 'aedificavit'?*
M.    *Aedifico significat 'aedes facio' vel 'exstruo.' Partes principales sunt extruo, -ere, extruxi, exstructum.*
P.     [continuing] *Frumentumque videre licet, nam copia magna intra aedes posita est quas aedificavit Iacchus. Quid est frumentum?*
M.    *Anglice est* corn.
P.     *Non intellego 'copia.'*
M.    *Scribite in libellis: copia, copiae, feminini generis.*
          [This sort of phrase will in this account henceforth be represented by the usual symbols, *copia, -ae (f.)*.] *Multum alicuius rei. Cumulus, acervus. Spectate cumulum librorum* [making a heap of books on his desk].
          All the equivalents are, of course, taken down by the boys in their notebooks.
P[2].   *Non bene intellego 'intra aedes posita est.'*
M.    *Quid est praesens tempus verbi?*
P.     *Pono.*
M.    *Quae sunt partes principales?*
P.     *Pono, -ere, posui, positum.*

| | |
|---|---|
| M. | [to a brighter boy] *Cape cretam et pone intra cistam.* [There is a chalk-box in the room.] *Ubi posita est creta?* |
| P. | *In cista posita est.* |
| M. | *Vel, intra cistam posita est.* |
| P. | [continuing] *Mus, frigus fugiens, in easdem irrepserat aedes qui sibi frumenti solus consumpsit acervum,* etc. |
| P². | *Quid est 'frigus'?* |
| M. | *Frigus est nomen, adiectivum est frigidus. Intellegitisne 'frigidus'?* |
| Class. | *Intellegimus.* |
| P. | *Frigidus sum.* |
| M. | *Frigus, -oris (n.). Quid facit mus?* |
| Class. | *Frigus fugit.* |
| P. | *Sed non intellego 'mus'.* |
| M. | *Est animal parvum quod feles amat edere.* |
| P. | *Non intellego 'feles'.* |
| M. | *Est animal quod canis non amat. Canis et feles semper inter se pugnant.* [The class may be asked to make the appropriate noises, thus: *Qualem sonum facit feles?*] *Scribite: mus, muris (m.) et feles, -is (f.). Et tu, Quinte, describe murem in tabula.* |
| P. | *Quid significat 'irrepserat'?* |
| M. | *Verbum est irrepo, -ere, -repsi, -reptum. Idem significat quod 'serpo.'* |
| P. | *Neque hoc intellego.* |
| M. | *Scitisne nomen 'serpens'?* |
| P². | *Ita. Licetne mihi describere?* |
| M. | *Licet tibi.* [Addressing the class] *Potestne serpens ambulare?* |
| Class. | *Minime vero.* |
| M. | *Cur non potest ambulare?* |
| P. | *Quia non habet pedes.* |
| M. | *Non igitur ambulat, sed serpit. Scribite: serpo, -ere, serpsi, serptum.* |
| P. | *Quid significat 'consumpsit'?* |
| P². | *Edit.* |

| | |
|---|---|
| M. | Bene. Scribite: consumo, -ere, -sumpsi, -sumptum. Mus sibi solus consumpsit acervum, id est unus mus totum edit acervum. Nemini dedit partem. |
| P. | [continuing] Occidit feles miserum saevissima murem frigora qui fugiens in easdem irrepserat aedes, etc. Quid significat 'occidit'? |
| P[2]. | Interfecit. |
| M. | Scribite partes principales: occido, -ere, -cidi, -cisum. |
| P. | Quid significat 'saevissima'? |
| M. | Quid est gradus positivus? |
| Class. | Saevus. |
| M. | Et gradus comparationis? |
| Class. | Saevus, saevior, saevissimus. |
| M. | Saevus est idem quod crudelis. Intellegitisne crudelis? |
| P. | Ita. Magister est crudelis. |
| M. | Minime vero. Ego sum benignus, immo vero benignissimus. Scribite in libellis: saevus, crudelis, hostilis, infestus. Omnia fere idem significant. |
| P. | [continuing] At felem canis hic infesto dente momordit, etc. Quid significat 'momordit'? |
| M. | Dentibus mordemus. |
| P. | Non intellego 'dentibus'. |
| M. | Dentes et lingua in ore sunt [he touches them]. Dens, dentis (m.); mordeo, -ere, momordi, morsum. Quibus instrumentis mordemus? |
| Class. | Dentibus mordemus. |

The master will now probably ask questions, thus:

| | |
|---|---|
| M. | Quis aedificavit aedes? |
| Class. | Iacchus aedificavit aedes. |
| M. | Quid aedificavit Iacchus? |
| Class. | Aedes aedificavit Iacchus. |
| M. | Quid intra aedes positum est. |
| Class. | Frumentum intra aedes positum est. |
| M. | Ubi positum est frumentum? |
| Class. | Intra aedes positum est frumentum. |
| M. | Cur in aedes irrepserat mus? |
| P. | Quia frigidus erat. |
| M. | Respondete omnes. |

*Class.* *Quia frigidus erat.*
*M.* *Quis murem occidit?*
*Class.* *Feles murem occidit.*
*M.* *Quem feles occidit?*
*Class.* *Murem feles occidit.*
*M.* *Et quis felem momordit?*
*Class.* *Canis felem momordit.*

And so on. These simple questions and answers form excellent practice both upon grammatical subject and object relations and upon the order of words. They also conduce to facility of expression upon the part of the boys and are, psychologically speaking, invaluable because the boys feel that they are finding the language easy to master in that they find themselves talking with such freedom. *Such a procedure as that outlined above is an essential part of the direct method.* The rest of the story will be treated in a similar way, and it is unnecessary to give a full account here, but perhaps it may be as well to show how some of the more difficult words are explained.

*Torta.* The master twists a piece of paper and says *chartam torqueo* and them tells a boy to draw the *cornua torta* on the board.

*Aerumnis confecta.* First *confectus* is explained as *vehementa affectus* and examples such as *dolore affectus sum* are given. These are readily understood from their similarity to English expressions. Then *aerumna* is paraphrased as *miseria* which is itself explained as the noun of *miser.*

*Cui tam pannosus amictus.* *Amictus* is *vestis,* which may be touched. *Pannosus amictus* is *vestis lacerata. Lacero* is explained by *seco* and demonstration. Then the English of *pannosus* may be asked for. Someone is sure to say 'ragged.' The construction is explained by saying that *erat* is to be understood and that *canis est mihi* = *canem habeo.*

*Caput rasus.* *Rasus* and *tonsus* are explained by demonstrating the actions expressed by the verbs *rado* and *tondeo.* Then the attention of the class may be drawn to the retained accusative by a few words in English. The teacher should never hesitate to give such an English explanation when necessary, though he need not do it at once. It is perhaps best to do so either at the end or beginning of a lesson in order not to dispel the Latin atmosphere by alternating repeatedly between Latin and English.

## § 20.

We conclude these hints to the teacher by giving a brief bibliography of some of the literature which has been published on the direct method.

*Classics and the Direct Method. An appeal to teachers*, by W. H. S. Jones. [Cambridge, Heffer.] 6*d*. net.

*Praeceptor*, by S. O. Andrew. [Oxford, Clarendon Press.] 2*s*. 6*d*. net.

*Some Practical Suggestions on the Direct Method of Teaching Latin*, by R. B. Appleton. [Cambridge, Heffer.] 2*s*.

*The School for the Reform of Latin Teaching*. Reports for 1911 and 1912. [Bell.] 1*s*. each. [See also articles in the *School World* for Nov., 1911; Sept. and Nov. and Dec., 1912; and a note in the correspondence columns of the same paper for April, 1913; also articles in the *Classical Review* for August, 1907, and June, 1908.]

*The Teaching of Latin at the Perse School*. Board of Education pamphlets No 20 (Wymans). 6*d*.

*Via Nova*, by W. H. S. Jones. [Cambridge University Press.]

*Teacher's Companion to Initium*

www.ingramcontent.com/pod-product-compliance
Lightning Source LLC
Chambersburg PA
CBHW020136130526
44590CB00039B/342